ECHOES OF THE BROKEN

IN YOUR MEMORIES I WROTE POETRY BUT I NEVER SEND IT (SELECTED A COLLECTION OF POEMS OF LOVE AND LOSS)

VAIBHAV NALAWADE

Dedicated To

To My Loved Once Even They Or They Don't...

Contents

Contents

Contents

Foreword

"Echoes of the Broken" is a collection of poems that delve into the depths of heartbreak and the lingering memories of lost love. Each verse is a reflection of the raw emotions and struggles of moving on from a relationship. Through the use of vivid imagery and powerful language, the author takes the reader on a journey of healing and self-discovery.

This book is dedicated to all those who have ever loved and lost. It is a reminder that we are not alone in our pain and that the echoes of our broken hearts will always be with us. The author writes with a sense of vulnerability and honesty, making this book relatable and powerful.

The subtitle of the book, "In your memories I write poetry but I never send it," speaks to the theme of unrequited love and the longing to be heard and understood. The poems within its pages are a testament to the power of words and the healing they can bring.

This collection of poetry is not only a work of art, but also a companion on the journey of healing and moving on. It is a reminder that even in the darkest of times, there is always hope and a chance for a new beginning.

Preface

Echoes of the Broken is a collection of poetry that explores the intricacies of love and heartbreak. The poems in this book are an outpouring of emotions that are raw and real, capturing the turmoil of a heart that has been shattered. The words in these pages are an attempt to make sense of a love that was lost, a relationship that was broken, and the scars that remain.

The author's dedication to their loved ones, even though they may not understand or reciprocate, is a testament to the power of love and the lengths we go to hold on to it. The book's subtitle, "In your memories I write poetry but I never send it," speaks to the private nature of these poems, written as a form of catharsis for the author rather than for the intended audience.

These poems are a reminder that love is not always easy, but it is always worth it. They are a testament to the resilience of the human heart and the capacity to love again. These are the echoes of the broken, a reflection of the pain and the beauty of a love that was, and the hope for a love that will be.

Write To Autor: vaibhavdn7@gmail.com

Instagram Personal: @vaibhavnalawade7

(https://www.instagram.com/vaibhavnalawade7/)

Instagram Poems: @vaibhavspoems

(https://www.instagram.com/vaibhavspoems/)

1. Thrilled by Your Touch

My love, I'm happy
When you are with me
Your looking daisy when moving
Baby your eyes looking, killer
Baby, I'm feeling thriller
I wanna grove with you
I feel like you're meth
I wanna be a pink man for you
I love your tasty lips
How I could take a breath
I want your breath in my breath
I never know your math
Your lips are hit for me
Your cozy lips on my lips
I feelin' like taking cuts on your lips
I take a trip with your hairs
I wanna play with your lose hairs
Our love has too many layers
Baby, i feel your aroma in an air
Baby, I love your all edges
Baby, you are teasing me
Baby you are making movements
I am lost in space no space in you & me
Baby your too much hot

I can't control to see you
Baby I love you

• 2 •

2. Falling in Love Again

After too many days
I was feeling on the top
After too many days
I was falling in the love again
I am falling down all the negativity
Just spreading the positivity
My heart is playing the melodies
Like your talks are remedies
Time is the priceless
Being here worth the cause
Everything comes at a cost
I never wanted to pay you the cost
That I had paid in the pain
Time made me stronger
Pain made me wise
With time what you realize
Realize it neither it could be a danger
Never feeling falling down
Calling from the town
I was like being in your town
Never down your crown

3. Ticking Clock Of Love

Tik tik tik boom tik tik tik
I was looking for double tik
At night clock is ticking
My heart beating slowly
I pick you so quick
You're in the wick
I seek me in your heart
Without you, I feel so sick
I just talking on paper
What I feel for you
My eyes are winking
In the sky, stars are blinking
I'm sinking for you in love
I'm thinking of linking
My heart to your heart
My art is inking for you
I feel you're my part
I feel I'm the you're part
But I don't know how to start
I am waiting for ringing my phone
I am in front of screen still feel alone
You're the apple of my eyes
You're the only star in my sky

4. Silent Longing

Why Everywhere Was Sorrow
My Mind Is Being Narrow
My Mind Is Boggle
Why No Smile On Your Face
How Could I Talk You
Looking At You Just For Your Smile
Are You Feeling Same What I Feel
Why Do I Think I Don't Fearless To Talk To You?
Why I Was Feeling Empty In Me?
I Was Being Enemy Of My Thoughts
Girl Your Beautiful Moves Killing In Me

5. Memories Flooded

I wrote thinking
That I will write and not
But Your Memories Flooded
I Thought One Last Time
Never be like this
If death ever comes to me
Don't be sorry in your heart
That I didn't tell you
How much I wanted you
I still want you
Your breath smells
I want you in words
It was my evening
My thoughts were on these philosophies
Now she doesn't even ask about my condition
Your answers remained incomplete in this heart
What are we even without you
We are also incomplete without you
Maybe now I can't even hope to answer
Heart Is Get Hurts

6. Round and Round With You

Round and Round With You
I Made Up Mistake
No Chance To Bounce Back
Baby I'm Mad At You
I Need To Be Grown Up
For One Time I'm Sleepy Owl
For Now I'm Being Lovely Owl
Baby Rounder On Your Hand
Baby, It's Now My Round
Baby I Wanna Be Take Round In Your City
Baby, I Wanna Be Around You
Baby, I Wanna Surround You With My Love

7. Me and My Pen

Me And My Pen
Me And My Pain
Never Goes Go
Time Goes Go
I Was Feeling In The Way
I'm On The High Wave
Stuck Like In One-Way
I Am Away From The All The Trash
I Finding Gateway To Get Away

8. Incomplete Without You

I don't write that story anymore
What I used to dream with you
I used to trust you not the world
I was afraid of losing you
I miss you
Moon also looks incomplete
As your words are incomplete
I am also incomplete without you
I Don't Need Why
I Need Just You
I Know What You Need
I Will Never Hold Back You
I Will Hold Your Hand Forever
I Am Living Somewhere
If your heart does
Give me a chance to hold your hand
To whom should I tell these stories
I don't have time for you
The pen just keeps writing
Past midnight
But still no sleep in my eyes
I am eating in the pictures of your memories

9. Holding Hands, Building Memories

It's all about you my love
Holding my hands
I want to hold your hands
Folding my memories
Building memories with you
I am waiting to loading me in your heart
I am fallin love with you
I'm trying to get closin to you
I'm loosing my control
I am coding for love
Encoding love messages for you
Love is whole thing for me
I am waiting to know your heart
Let me know how time go
Let me say I love you
Let me go my heart is craving your answers
Let me show you these to understand

10. Broken Relationships

Drowned in the battle of thoughts
Don't know how many people got hurt by thoughts
What kind of pain is this that has no end
What kind of story is this that has no end
Don't know how many pains I wrote
Tell me the stories of your heart by singing
I haven't heard the thoughts of your heart
You don't want to come at this rate
How is our luck
We live in the same city
Without each other
We will never meet again
We live for hearts of stone
We kept on filling the cracks of broken relationships
We kept singing like travelers
Don't remember the things of yesterday

11. Pearl In Kashmir

I'm seeing that one girl
She is looking like a pearl
She is shining like a sunset peak
I wanna collect all your gems
From your jewel
I am feeling too cool
Like I am on the heritage of Kashmir
It's too hot to handle
My mind is getting boggle
Your look gorgeous from every angle like an angel
I feel you're coming from the heaven of the earth
I wanna spend time with you in the vale of Kashmir
I wanna do dinner with you in candles
To see the shine on your face
I'm writing this chorus for you
Forgive me for what i say
I'm seeing sleep in your eyes
Let's take break in the heaven of kashmir
I'm losing my conscious consciously

12. Going Slowly Lonely

I'm listening that deeply
Like song of my favourite singer
You're grooving on me like a my favourite rap
I'm going slowly slowly lonely
But I never feel lonely
I need some more dedication
For meditation
I'm going slowly slowly lonely
But I never feel lonely
I'm thinking about only you
I feel that closely
I'm spending time with lovely night

13. Imprisoned Heart

How to let go of this heart
Who is imprisoned here love or relationship
This story would not have ended
This relationship doesn't progress
I Don't Know How Much I Waited
I Am Moving Calculated
I Forgot The What I Created
Every Moment With You I Celebrated
I Am Addicted To You
Everything Is Included
I Feel Like I Am A Tired
I Feel Like It's One-Sided
I Feel Everything Is Ended
I Feel Like I'm A Dead

14. I Miss You

I miss you
I remembering that one day
That you kissed me in the dark
You're holding back my hands
I feel our life will be light up
You'll be with me for life long
You're chasing my lips
I'm feeling it like my life eclipse
I miss you i feel you just kiss me
All the mess in my head
Even I can't wirte one word ahead

15. Healing Wounds

My wounds will heal with time
I found medicines but no use
It sounds good someone will be in my heart
No matter how much you hurt me
Someone will replace your memories in my heart
I'm still on the ground to see you
Since you left I found myself more than you
No, any connecting love threads
Still, I think you deserve to forgive
I'm changing my traits
You will never find me what you have seen
Scenes are changing my mind is changing
My wounds healed with time
Someone has filled my heart?

16. Lost in Flaws

I am not close to anyone
I have seen too many flaws
My life never glows
I've no any life clue
I stick with entertainment like a glue
I've no any willpower
I'm not taking any showers
Water is running like my thoughts
I was ruining my life
I never tell the truth to myself
I never win the tail
I never understood what to tell
Feelin me living in hell

17. Balcony Talks

I am standing in the balcony
I'm finding ways to ways to talk to you
To listen to your melodious voice
I am trying to talk to you
I'm missing you whole day
I am trying to knock your heart
If you are with me then every day becomes a festival
Wish you were with me today
I get your company
No one but you take care of yourself
I see another dream of you
Everything is fine, there is no pain in you
If you are happy then i am writing on the pages of happiness

18. Lost Without You

I hope I'll find peace
My head is soaring
Talking just not goes pain
My heart is painless
If you can take off the pain
Let me say something to my pen
I feel lost in my path at what a cost
I feel girl I need you
I hope I'll find you in my life

19. Mystery and Victory

She feels her devotion to close one's happiness
She is finding her ecstasy in a close one
I never know her chemistry
I every day knowing her as a mystery
I feel you're my destiny
I want you through my misery
To make my victory
After my purpose being with you it's my victory

20. Raindrops And Tears

Eyes close tears drop
Weather changes raindrops
In the rain, I could not find my tears
Raindrops and my tears are the same
How do they know my pain
But I never share my pain with anyone
It doesn't mean I don't have any pain
I am not weak cause pain makes me stronger
I feel younger
My life is no longer
But I live life purposefully
All they are gone you also gone
Still my pen with me
My life is scatter
Like rain scatter on my face
I am looking at her face like
Passing clouds of rain

21. Wounds And Purpose

Back in the day, there is a way
Rocking the day but I am away
I am knocking on the door of the heart
Talking to my heart gets hurt
Wounds on my heart still I am here
I looked down nothing found
I found my wounds that never healed
I only owned sorrows and notorious thoughts
Back in the past my life was too much worst
There is no any hope
Dope in my hand
My eyes wrinkled face sprinkled
All my sorrows linked to the stars
I get scared no one know
I am still here with my wounds
I found a purpose in life
I accepted all my wounds
Now my life is carry forwarded(dead)
I get new birth for life for love

22. Dreaming Of Losing You

Sometimes I feel too strange
I feel something different
Today I have a dream
In which you left me
I feel so alone that's why
I won't keep listening to you
You want to leave me
I don't want to lose you
I want to be close to you
When you close your eyes
I want to be there with you
I want to see the world through your view

23. Falling In Love

I don't know don't know
What to do how to do
I am in a flood of emotions
I am not taking any action
I want to give a motion to you
I want to give action to our life
I am finding devotion in you
I found devotion in love
I see glow on your face
I feel flow in your voice
I want to go with your flow
I want you more than the you
I love you more than you know
I am in love with you
I wanna know side your side
Sometimes I feel I am hiding my feelings
Every time I see you
I feel fallen love with you
I don't wanna miss you
I wanna be with you
Every time I see you
I feel fallen love with you

24. Love's Riddle

Sometimes I feel our love is a riddle
I am in the middle of love & friendship
Our love is on the needle
How should I balance
Sometimes I feel unsure
How can I make our love pure?
I have hopes for our future
I will get all the answers
When you'll independent
My heart is looking to you

25. Love Umbrella

No expectations living on the hopes
I am writing this for you & dope
No, any explanation just accelerating my thoughts
Just expressing my heart talks to you
I am climbing on the purpose rocks
I am trying to break friendship blocks
But every time i get friendship shocks
My love is warped in the box
It's on you to unwrap the love box
Talking my heart shit to the my pen
I just gone through the pain
I am counting the rain drops
Finding the love umbrella with in you

26. Friendship Bricks

Life is never been easy
I became lazy I want break it
I feel love is ecstasy
I never want sipin hennessey
For me all these are freak
They are giving me free tricks
I am taking the risks
To build love on friendship bricks

27. Missed Embrace

I miss you
I wanna kiss you
By holding your hand on your neck
I wanna touch your soft cheeks
I wanna feel your lips trough my lips
I wanna do pillow fight with you
I wanna do unstoppable love on you
Guitar is playing low & high
I am listening to your lovely voice
I miss you
I wanna kiss you
I wanna feel your lips trough my lips

28. Confession

No way to say you
I wanna say you I love you
I just saying myself
I love herself
I wrote this for you
I don't know when you see
I don't know when you understand
I wanna stand with you
Love in my heart fire in my words
I was thinking
How could I say I love you
I don't know why I stuck with you
I want to know why I am stuck in the loop
How should I stop this loop
I just want unstoppable love

29. Insomnia Love

I was kissing you
And my sleep break
I was trying to fall in sleep
Every time I try I fall in love with you
No sleep in my eyes
My mind says to me
I want to talk to you
I want to look deep into your eyes

30. Intermittently

My life went on intermittently
I write thinking for you
I used to find words for you
I write to you every night
Rose in my hand
I Want Just Break Friendship Band
Flying in the sky yet living on the ground
When we meet the moments will be grand

31. Head in the Sand

My Head Is Soring
I Feel Like Dead
What's My Deed
How To Feed My Purpose
I Am Trying To Read My Destiny
My Life Is Going Forward
Sometimes I Feel I Holding Back Myself
It Seems Like I Backward My Destiny
I Feel Like I Am On The End
I Am In The House Of Sand
Sand Can Fall Any Time
To Bury Me In The Sand Before The Time

32. Crazy Thoughts

I got some crazy thoughts
I am being like the craziest person
This is not my persona
I don't care how you pursue it
I rarely write like this
When I write I don't care, anyone
No more feelings for anyone
I don't care even if you hurt me
Once upon a time, there is one heart
Who cares for every heart
That was the art of that heart
I lived my life with this heart
But i left this heart far away from me
Serving love get back love for me
But i don't get back my love
This heart never expected to love me back
Even i never expecting to love me back
But they go by holding me back
I am just folding back my memories
I never play with anyone's heart
I am undefeated for the entire life
But i lost by winning in life
It feels like a my life-changing
I feel like everything falling down

Heart calling back me
To live my life with heart
But i lack the love how could i live with heart
Still trying to live with a heart

33. No Connections

My phone list full of contacts
No, any context to contact
Too many friends in contacts
No one is there to connect
I have thousands of contacts
I got thousands of thoughts
No one is there to hear my chaos
Gram is full of DMs but no one is to connect
I got no friends to talk love
I got her as a friend
But she has no time
I am busy in making a rhyme

34. Beyond The Dreams

Feels like a psychedelics
Who is the my colleagues
I am on the high waves
You're on the highways
I am looking at you babes
Eyes got trap on you babes
Where are the my friends
Where is the my love
Finding you in the my dream world
Understanding you in the real world
Caring you like queen of world
King of the your world
You are the mighty
Over the top your beauty
Underdog in the limelight
You matter for me
Beyond the dreams
Increasing my love
Thanks to god for you
Chaos still in the my mind
Hesitation still to tell you in my mind

35. Heart Of Mine

What could i tell
I found the girl
I ever wish i will
I never see that girl
Part of my heart
I am giving it you
I am living you
I am living the love
I feel like i seen you from the heaven
I wish i meet you from day one
The part of my heart is waiting for you
I am giving my heart to you
I loving like a you
My lips singing song for you
My heart is looking for you
My heart is loving for you

36. Lies in Love

I stuck at same situation
Every time i love
I am losing my mind
No time to rewind
I feel my life is a just lie
I am looking in the your eyes
I am feeling so high high
But all the time i got your lies
I forgot everything my love
I gave everything to my love
I feel alone tonight my love
I feel to move on my love

37. Life's Equation

My life is a life lie
No girls no high
No question my life is question
I am solving life's equation
No faith shaitan in my mind
I need one more lifeline
I am smoking weed on the high
Life goes life like fly
I am drawing the lines on table
I am snorting the lines
I am popping the pills
Sip in sipin hennessey
I am killing my pain
I am fooling in the game
I don't wanna live anymore
Who care i am being real
This is not game of horn or howl
It's game of ethics in the delusion bowl

38. Ego Girl

I got that ego girl
I got love versus time
I always preferred the time
Forget all this girl
With the time relations are faded
It seems like your truth is a naked
I feel you are to mean
There is no any scene
You are doing cheap tactics
I feel like a cheap thrills
I never call this tactics
I just laugh on this cheap thrills
You never know the true love
Being physical with me it's not a love
It's your lust bust to this thought
It's not a true love for me
They said time is the money
I paid the price for it
I feel things are the priceless

39. Astronauts

Roses in the space
Thrones in the case
Roots in the base
Astronauts in the space
When i see her in reality
I am feeling in zero gravity
No more i live in reality
I am going beyond infinity
I am calculating your gravity
Mathematically to see your probability
I am looking outside of the galaxy
To see the roses I am following you closely
I am looking at you loosely
She loves Gucci bags
I wanna be your groupie
With specs, she looking a cutie pie
I wanna just say hi

40. Roses and Love

Roses are not to smell
No time to smell roses
Roses are the pink
Cheeks are the red
She is the ahead of me
What she thinks
I wanna just drink
I am to much shrink
When i she her my eyes blink
How could i link

41. Forever

I don't need why
I need just you
I know what you need
I will never hold back you
I will hold your hand forever
I am living in somewhere

42. Addicted To You

I don't know how much I waited
I am moving calculated
I forgot what I created
Every moment with you I celebrated
I am addicted to you
Everything is included
I feel like I am a tired
I feel like it's one-sided
I feel everything is ended
I feel like I am a dead

43. Twice the Sight

I was like a like in the house
I was seeing the twice
Something like you on the table
Now tables turn
I am gonna be burn
Be confident as you are
What I worth on the earth
Like a rebirth on the earth

44. One-Sided Love

It's a bad thing that we are good friends
You never feel for me never mind
I feel for you, you are not my friend
I feel my love is one-sided
You decided not to be with me
I decided to love you
My mind changed that
You are not my friend anymore
I thought deeply I feel for you
After the sunset diamonds won't shine
After the friendship love won't start
After the sunshine diamonds shine again
How much I love you time will tell you again

45. Lonely Turn

To many friends
No, any close friend
They never know me as a friend
My life is like at the end
No excuses
I might be wrong
What could I do what I do
How do I do
My life takes turns

46. All busy

I am busy thinking about you
You patrol with your best friend
You don't bother to understand me
Everyone seems corrupt
No longer takes the pain of understanding
Your destination is standing on lies
I stand by the truth of our love
You broke her dream of being big
There's nothing to lose now
But there are too many memories to cry

47. Living For Two Moments

Let it happen with you too
Keep happening even after you
Your words remain in my heart
Those who make me miserable
Why do my hands tremble even with you
Let your love stumble
From friend to love, from love to defeat
I want to live with you
Get lost in your memory
I want to laugh with you just for a second
I want to cry with you, I want to lose myself in your arms
I want to sleep with you in this open sky
It is right to live for two moments with you

48. Beauty In Distance

You are so beautiful
I am compelled to write about you
As beautiful as you
You are far away
Now things are not like before
These nights don't last
How those your words
Makes me cry when I remember
I keep getting lost in your thoughts
There are many questions in the heart

49. A Desire to be Free Again

Not angry with anyone
I'm just angry with myself
I am a little shy
Tryin' to fly a little high
I write how I don't know
But there is a desire in my heart to be free again
I'm taking myself out of sight
Whenever I see ok I can't see you anymore
How can I say that I am still the same, only you have changed
Again hope in the mind
Everything will be like before just you see

50. Unrealized Memories

He sings the song but i don't
Living together but not realizing
I don't remember things
Let's not see each other
I'm lost in these memories
I have learned to laugh from these memories
Don't make me cry now
I've been ready for this too

51. Unseen Beauty

Saw the sunburn every day

But you never see it

In the dark night under the beautiful moonlight

I saw your smile and fell in love with it

I'm with you when no one else

Maybe meet again with this excuse

It doesn't take long for the seasons to come and the seasons to go

I am not a liar but not a proof of the truth

Your little things make my heart happy

I'm Not An Perfect My Mind Is Boggle

I just tie flowers of your praise

Your beauty cannot be described by words

All the ages are spent in making heart to heart

52. Remembered Smiles

You had brought from with love
Remembering your smile keeps my heart entertained
Oh it was a few moments, won't you get it again
Will remember that for the rest of my life
Don't give up trying
But I didn't understand anything
Looks like maybe my bad karma
I was under some other illusion
Maybe now it seems that was my religion
There is only hope in the heart
I Will Climb The Top

53. Broken Inside

I am the river in myself
Why doesn't flow
With my own dreams
Why don't you say anything
Inside with myself
The whole sea is broken inside
How can I tell why everyone seems barren to me?
Broken from the inside is the angriest philosophy,
I am not from home, you are free, I am not free
I was broken inside
The world was angry with me
The river flows from the sea
What I used to tell myself

54. Crown of My Heart

Not that crown of head
I am not dependent on unnecessary things
You are my crown
Why I Always Feeling Like These Days
Why I Am Gonna Miss You I Want To Kiss You
I'm not mean
Everything has a meaning
I will come everything means joyful

55. Patience and Felony

How many sheets of goodness
How much did they show my patience
Yet never appreciate them
Now maybe they'll wait till my grave
All These Are Fallacy Like An Felonies
Looking for a greater life
There is a desire in my mind to be better every day
Broken from the inside at every step, most liar
Asking myself why am I grumpy with the world
How you punished me
Where do I find my freedom?

56. Ashes and Emptiness

If it is not complete then destroy it
Sorry if offended
Burn everything to ashes
Eat everything to ashes
I am not in talks, nor in the night
Don't sleep alone with me
Cry make me cry lose me
Don't talk to me

57. Unsatisfied Longings

How many things used to happen here
Money does not fill the mind
Find happiness in your body
Still not satisfied
Your wish lives in the heart
Believe it or not, you are my life
Now I need some recognition
Which your name is
I was walking away
I was distancing myself

58. Flowing Like a River

You flow like a river
What can you say?
I got lost in your childish talk
With you, I got drowned in these feelings
This journey looks great
Just a little regret in my heart
Untold things that you heard
Weave such webs of words
I feel in you

59. Broken Promises of Love

Why see the pain
See the wound why the ointment should be made
You are never with me even after being near
So why make false promises of love
Why tell stories of hazy love
I am scared, why did the hand become a hammer
How to collect the pieces of this scattered heart
How long did this flower bear the pain
When will these withered flowers forget the pain
When will these withered flowers bloom
When will this flower bring a smile on your face
I am on his way, my heart will get relief
I have so much love for you in my heart

60. Vanishing Faces

Why are all the missing faces here
Stars are not visible at night
Bottles are getting empty at night
It's been a long time since I heard your abuse
Empty heart, empty road, black nights
My black deeds are just emptying the jam
In your name, jam will be broken in sip n sip Hennessy.
Now you won't even remember my name

61. Forgotten Memories

You don't even talk to me
Maybe you don't even remember me
You don't even know who i am
I am yours, you never thought of this
These things left in the wind
Even my life is present for you
It doesn't cost you
Love felt the mind
You put your mind
How Can I Say I Am Done
All the heads are lying in the house
We sit in your memories

62. Unseen Love

She is sending photos
Tattoos on her hands
Cut seven on her hand
My heart with you
My soul wanders around you
How special you are to me
You don't even know
I'm breathing
Because you are in my heart
If you don't find me in this world
So understand that I have not lived in this world
You Never Know Me
76 The Illusion of Perfection
How nice it would be if
No one gets jealous
Everyone get along
No one should ever lose their loved ones
Never make anyone cry
No one ever cry
The world should not drown in sorrow
I know the truth
Tell the truth
This story is not liked in the world
Looks good only on paper

VAIBHAV NALAWADE

The world ran away from the truth
I run away from my work
Why i don't want to work hard

63. Toxic Love

Life doesn't end like this
There was a rift with loved ones
Relationships become Toxic
Creosol full in you
Your body became Toxic
Should I sell my soul to the devil
Can i cherish you again in my life
You took me out of home or heart
Whether you see me again right or not,
There are deceptions and opportunities here
How many will you stop

64. Unheard Words

There is trust, there is love too
But never listen to my words
Dream world, dream house
Want to meet you
Feel like I'm getting buried
How long my patience
Maybe you will come to my senses on my grave
I'm sick of myself
You Don't Wanna Talk
Even food does not come down the throat
I don't even want to go away from you
What about me to you
You yourself are unaware
I'm getting impatient day by day

65. Alone in the City

Lost me

it's too noisy here

silent i

I'll try to do a few things

This city is full of people

I meet people every day in this city

Still alone in this city

Found quite a few people who don't call themselves in the city

Got everything except our own in this city

Dreams come true in this city

I am writing the story of reality on paper

Sometimes the unwanted path is visible in reality

My pen with paper

My relationship with Shahi deepened

Papers do not hide my pain

The paper knows my deep secret

66. Reflections On Relationships

I keep coming and going through these routes
the paths of which your home is
May I ever turn my way to your home
I'm deep in thought
can I give her a call
should I ask him how he is
what should I do I ask him
how is your heart
Relationships here of all heart
Relationships are being weighed here with money
how do we intervene
How to fill the gap in these relationships
some relationship is going well
Is my art drowning these relationships
I say that I am fine alone
For the first time, I am getting peace of mind

67. Scars of Love

The scars on the heart don't fade away
It took a long time for the wounds to heal
Don't know how many nights passed without you
I want to erase the scars but I can't
These roses freshen the wounds
What I already forgot
Rose petals hurt more than thorns
This life was spent with wounds only
I wasn't even responsible before
like I'm responsible today
I had committed the crime of love
Living away from you is his punishment
If you see scars
If you understand my stories
So I still want you
I'm sitting waiting for you

68. Alone in the Sky

I was watching the sky
When I saw the moon, I remembered you
So I started writing
Alone I was writing
What you think is not my secret
What you say is not in my heart
You don't listen to what I tell you
You don't read what I write
It's, not a distance anymore
We don't stay on the ground
If you were not here, I would have felt your absence
Sometimes my eyes become moist
I was watching the sky
alone I was writing
Show me a shooting star
And I was writing
I am not lucky to meet you
Will this fate change?

69. Echoes of You

Tell the truth or lie
or anything I say
How can I live without your support
Don't want to write more about you
When I remember you, my pen does not stop
I've probably said it a hundred times
Even after that, I wrote a lot
After that, I suffered a lot
I can't see the words on your face
I do not tell you about my cities
The mind is not amused by the words of strangers
No love in other's words
How many years have passed
We have never met in all these years
We talked a lot
All those things remained on paper
I remembered you so I dm you
I got your reply
But I have no words left to reply
So I started writing again
One Tap Everything Fade Up
What We Made Up
I Want To Be The Part Of You Till The Death
But God Knows Our Faith

VAIBHAV NALAWADE

God Knows

• 73 •

70. Regrets

I made wrong decisions
I didn't think about you
Didn't listen I took care of you
I have not seen your relationship with me
Now those moments are over
You too have moved on
But we can't forgive ourselves
We keep learning from life
This heart was infatuated with your love
This heart had become used to you...
Every night I think
What should I do Message you that I miss you
But I would not have dialed your number
I don't even watch WhatsApp daily
I Wanna Know What's Up
I Miss You Like
Missing Rain In Sea Shell
Wishing the Best For You But I Fail
I try to fix my mistakes